Table of Contents

Overview: What you can expect to learn from this book

This book contains all of the basics that you need to know about blockchain: what it is, how it came into being, why it is important, what its impact can be, and how it can be used (and is currently in use) in the contemporary world. Apart from these basic discussions, we have also included useful definitions throughout the book to aid your reading, as well as lightly technical discussions of how blockchain coins and tokens are stored, the risks of blockchain, challenges facing the adoption, use, and security of blockchains, and noteworthy news stories about recent developments in the blockchain space.

When it comes to the discussion of current uses and applications of blockchain technologies, this discussion invariably gravitates towards talking about how blockchain is impacting banking, finance, investment, and real estate, because these are the industries that stand to be changed (and benefitted) the most from blockchain solutions. However, even industries such as education, security, and social media are being forever impacted by startups working in this field. As a result, as more and more industries become more and more data-intensive, and as blockchain tech becomes more and more widespread, the tools and technologies that use it become inherently tied to concerns about data security. This is one of the reasons that decentralized blockchain ledgers are an exciting new area of discovery because it deals with novel and creative ways to store information, to make transactions, to perform functions, and to establish trust.

All of these factors make blockchain extremely adaptable to environments that require high levels of security, whilst having to deal with many unknowns at the same time. So in addition to the topics planned for discussion as outlined above, we will make sure to go into a little detail discussing opportunities and challenges related to blockchain across all of these industries.

Please bear in mind that, although this is a beginner's guide to blockchain, our coverage of the topic is quite comprehensive. We will talk not only about the technical aspects and applications of blockchain technology, but we will also include coverage of other important and relevant issues such as obstacles to adoption and legal and risk-related issues to give the reader as complete a picture of everything as possible.

Introduction: Where we are today

Throughout human history, countless inventions and discoveries have been made. Some of these developments have been minor, some have been major, some have been short-lived, and others have been more important and longer-lasting. In fact, there are certain developments that have taken place over the course of history that have been so vitally important to humanity as a whole that it can be argued that those inventions or discoveries were the sole factor behind all of humankind collectively making progress and taking an important, visible, and everlasting leap forward.

To illustrate with an example, think about how the creation of fertilizers and farming equipment allowed for the exponential growth of food output from fixed pieces of land, without which the world would not have been able to support the populations we see across the globe today. It was hardly a few hundred years ago that economists and scientists portended the end of population growth, citing the fact that food production only grew at numerical rates (doubling or tripling every certain number of years), while populations grew at exponential rates (growing to the power of two or more in the same period of time).

This obviously meant that, sooner or later, there wouldn't be enough food to feed everybody, unless more food could be extracted from fixed pieces of land every year. Luckily, that is exactly what happened: science delivered heavy farm equipment, fertilizers such as ammonia, and other improvements in farming practices so that food harvests could keep up with population growth rates, and more people could be sustained on the same area of land as before. Without these developments, the world would be a very, very different place today, and it would be an understatement to say that advances in farming have been anything but a victory of human achievement that will be marveled at for all time to come.

Similarly, the creation of penicillin, antibiotics, the introduction of ocean freight and air travel, the steam engine (which was the driving force behind the Industrial Revolution), and, more recently, the sharing of information in the Information Age that was made possible by the creation of transistors and microchips, have all irreversibly changed the world, that too for the better. As a result of all of these innovations, we are all more connected, better off, healthier, and have better, easier, and cheaper access to goods and services than anyone has ever had in the past.

When it comes to the information age, things have progressed at breakneck pace ever since the first dot-com wave in the early to mid-90s. Everything from the UI tools and technologies that define how we interact and interface with technology, to banking and payment solutions, have all changed dramatically over the last 20 years or so.

The same can be said of basic email and social networks, not to mention advancements that have been made in the fields of big data analysis and AI, both of which impact everything from online search to helping with governance. Collectively, we've gone from basic solutions for all of the above to having intricate software services that combine different aspects of technology to deliver robust, effective, value-added, and seamless services to billions of people all over the world.

Big data: extremely large data sets that can be analyzed computationally to reveal patterns, trends, and associations, especially relating to human behavior and interactions.

AI: Artificial intelligence is intelligence exhibited by machines, rather than humans or other animals, and it is an increasingly popular area of mathematical and computational research.

However, with progress come new challenges. Big data, AI, the ability of governments to implement mass surveillance initiatives, and the ubiquity of technology all around us pose serious ethical questions and technological challenges for anyone living in the 21st century.

Where do you draw the line between legal and illegal surveillance? How can private, personal data, exabytes of which is generated on a daily basis (that's 10 followed by 17 zeros!), be kept safe, secure, and private? How important is data integrity and privacy? How can we trust companies and governments when data usage collection and manipulation practices are not transparent? Where is the world headed when it comes to the role of big corporations or governments in society, and their relationships with private users or individuals?

It is with this interesting yet challenging background in mind that we will discuss the blockchain, which is so much more than the latest tech fad. It is, in the opinion of many tech gurus and subject area experts, the next giant leap for all of mankind, something that will have as great an impact on us and our children as farming and healthcare developments had on our great-great-grandparents a century ago. We are literally in a new Information Age, but this time, although things are still driven by circuits, binary computations, and better integration of technology into our everyday lives, it is very likely that the blockchain will forever change the way we do things.

Ok, I'm convinced. This is clearly a pretty big deal. So what exactly IS the Blockchain? If you read on then you will find out!

Chapter 1: Some History

Although the concept behind a permanent, decentralized ledger such as the blockchain was first discussed as early as 1991, the first actual blockchain implementation was designed by Satoshi Nakamoto in 2008. It was his design that was used as the underpinning technology that runs the digital currency now known as bitcoin.

The blockchain that Mr. Satoshi engineered serves as the public ledger for all bitcoin transactions, but we should be very clear about what we are talking about here: bitcoin, a digital currency worth roughly $16,000 today (with a total market value of all bitcoin exceeding $500bn), runs on blockchain technology, not the other way around.

The best known blockchain is that for Bitcoin. A site showing all this information is *blockchain.info*. Another well known blockchain is the *Ethereum* blockchain. Ethereum is the second most valuable cryptocurrency. You can see the Ethereum blockchain, as it is modified, by visiting *etherscan.io/blocks*. Using this, you can see the information contained in the Ethereum blockchain. If you click on any number in the Height column you are taken to another webpage with information about the contents of that block. As you read this book you will learn what a block in blockchain is.

The technology that allows bitcoin to serve as a digital currency, as a store of value, and as a medium of exchange is blockchain, because bitcoin transactions are recorded in a blockchain ledger. This means blockchains are not limited to running bitcoin; rather, blockchain applications span the entire gamut of finance, trade, healthcare, records management, legal operations, gaming, probability, online exchanges, and more. You will learn how important this is later.

Chapter 2: Money, Cryptocurrency, Blockchain

Money

You may well ask what is money? : Money is nearly as old as humanity. Many books have been written on its history. A brilliant book is *The Ascent Of Money: A Financial History Of The World* by *Niall Ferguson*. Money has to be both a store of value and a means of exchange. In the past the following have been used as money: gold, cattle, silver, beads, and salt. No matter what its form, money has to execute these two essential functions. In addition, there has to be trust that these roles can be fulfilled by the money.

Cryptocurrency

Cryptocurrency?: Using the encryption techniques of mathematics and computing, we can create money that is called cryptocurrency. Using these techniques, we can transfer funds and verify that the transfer has occurred. Independence of governments and central banks is an important feature of all true cryptocurrencies. For this reason, they are said to be **decentralized**.

Many important banks are getting increasingly involved with the same technology that underlies cryptocurrncy.However, any currency arising from their endeavours will not be true cryptocurrency as it will be controlled by these banks. Cryptocurrency's strongest and most dedicated advocates are determined that there shall be no such centralization.

How have cryptocurrencies developed?: The best known cryptocurrency is Bitcoin. It has been the recipient of publicity, fame and hype. The general public has been mesmerized by its extraodinary increase in value. They have been bedazzled by tales of extraordinary wealth generated with Bitcoin, for those who were lucky enough to acquire Bitcoin, when they were cheap.

 They are rapidly realizing that Bitcoin is genuine money, despite its novely. In addition to Bitcoin, there are a great many other cryptocurrencies, and many of these have also had a huge increase in their dollar value. Legitimate business and government are pursuing an increasing involvement with cryptocurrency. Despite critics, and there are many, the market in these currencies is thriving. The market capitalization of all cryptocurrencies in December 2017 exceeded $500,000,000,000! In August 2017, the market capitalization was $120,000,000,000!

In mid-December 2017, a check on the Internet showed there to be more than 1,300 cryptocurrencies. If you are interested in cryptocurrency, there is a website *coinmarketcap*. If you visit this site, you will be intrigued at the information there, about most cryptocurrencies.

How is Cryptocurrency related to Fiat Currencies and Stocks? : The currencies we use in daily life, such as the dollar, renminbi, euro, and yen, are called 'fiat currencies', by those in the cryptocurrency world. Despite the word 'currency' appearing as part of the word cryptocurrency, there is greater similarity between cryptocurrencies and the stocks and shares of the stock market than between cryptocurrency and fiat currencies. Purchasing some cryptocurrency, gets you some of the coin for that cryptocurrency, this acts like a technology stock, and a digital entry in a ledger called a *blockchain*. Soon, we will have far more to say about this last term.

Blockchain

GENERAL LEDGER

Purchases	Credits
Assets	Wages
Revenue	Profits
Losses	Cash Flow
Dividends	Risk
	Equity

What is a blockchain?: In the previous paragraph we indicated that a blockchain is a digital ledger. A blockchain can be formally defined as a continuously-growing list of records that are linked together and secured using advanced cryptography. In this way, a blockchain is literally a chain of blocks. In fact, the terms 'block chain' and 'blockchain' are used interchangeably. Each record in the list of a blockchain's chain is called a block, and it contains very specific pieces and types of information. Each block usually contains some sort of pointer as a link to the previous block, a timestamp, and transaction data, which can take many different forms (additional details on this will be discussed when we talk about the different types of blockchains currently in operation in the market).

To put it another way, a blockchain is much like a database in which each entry is linked to the previous and next entry, and the information contained therein cannot be changed, once a block with certain data has been added to the chain. Depending on the chain you are looking at, there are often useful exploring tools that allow you to scan transaction data, which is true to the design of blockchain as being open, public, and verifiable.

> *A **blockchain** is a continuously growing list of records called blocks, which are linked and secured using cryptography.*

Blockchains are by their inherent design, resistant to modification of the data they contain. This allows blockchains to record transactions between different parties efficiently and in a way that is not only verifiable but also permanent. Once information in a block is recorded, the data in the block cannot be altered after-the-fact without altering of all subsequent blocks by having a majority of nodes (discussed soon) on the network agreeing to the change.

This makes unfair or illegal actions almost impossible to carry out. A hacker who wished to alter information on the blockchain would have to be able to control every node. This security is one of the most profound and useful characteristics of the blockchain.

Because they are designed to be permanent and verifiable, blockchains are particularly suitable for recording events, drawing up agreements, maintaining medical records, fundraising, and keeping track of other records such as identity management and transaction processing. We will talk more about blockchain applications later in the book.

Chapter 3: How blockchains work

What is needed to run a blockchain?

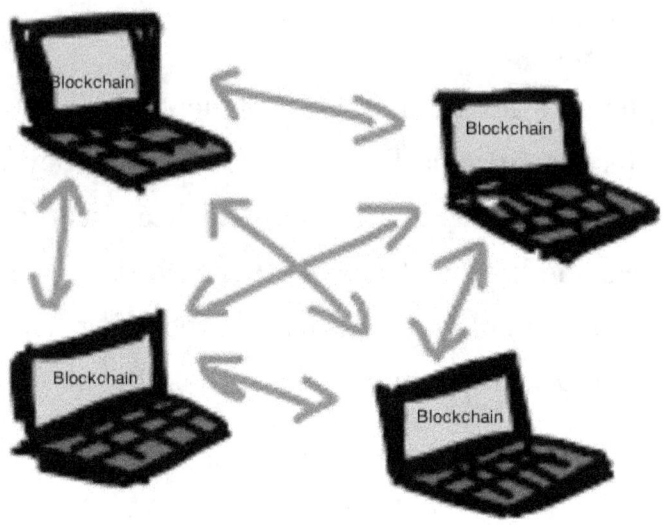

A blockchain can be likened to a huge spreadsheet, distributed over a giant computer network. <u>The computers in this network are called *nodes*</u>; we talked about nodes in the last chapter. Each node has a copy of this spreadsheet, which is the blockchain. In the grossly simplified picture above there are four nodes. In actual fact, the number of nodes may run into the thousands. The Bitcoin blockchain has over 5,000 nodes.

Several times an each hour, this spreadsheet or ledger is updated. Consequently, the information in the ledger (blockchain) is real-time and correct. The interaction of the nodes is determined by what are called *protocols*. Very simply, protocols are software rules.

A most important feature of blockchains is that each node has the entire ledger. This feature makes the blockchain secure. Because every node possesses all the records, there is no centralization of records. If you inspect the blockchain, you will find that the records are public and on any node. Hackers love to concentrate their attacks on one weak or vulnerable point. If a hacker desired to launch a raid on a blockchain, they would need to successfully attack each node of the whole network, in order to be successful, something that, currently, is impossible.

Miners

No discussion about blockchain proceeds very far before the topics of *mining* and *miners* arise, but what is bitcoin or blockchain mining?

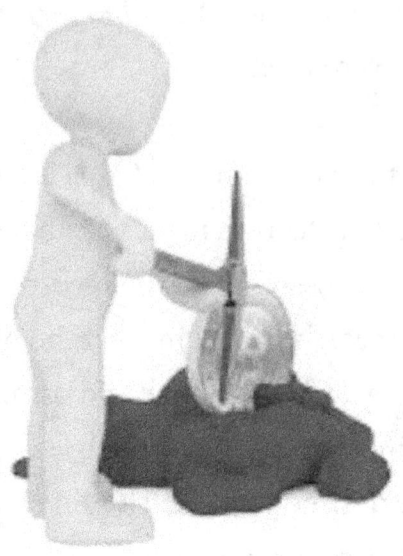

Miners on a blockchain are nodes that produce blocks by solving what are called *proof of work* problems. If a miner produces a block that is approved by an electronic consensus of nodes then the miner is rewarded with coin.

Bitcoin and other blockchain protocols run on a system of recorded transactions that are open for public reading and writing. Transactions can be aggregated and published by anyone, as long as they can show that they put in enough effort to do so. To show that sufficient effort went into creating or aggregating a transaction, users on the network have to solve difficult cryptographic puzzles.

Once the solution to a specific puzzle that ties one block to the next is verified on the network as having been solved by a specific user, that user is rewarded for creating the next block on the chain by receiving bitcoins (if we are talking about users on the bitcoin network) or other digital assets (depending on the type of blockchain we are talking about; examples are given below).

So the user who reached the puzzle solution first is rewarded with new coins, and each solution and the transactions on the block that were used to verify the solution are used by the system to create the next problem that needs to be solved.This means that solving successively difficult numerical challenges means the problems get much, much harder over time, and solving them takes a lot of computing and electrical power, meaning it is a high-energy process that is not easy nor cheap to do.

The picture above shows a vast array of machines, all mining for Bitcoins!

Mining is the process of adding records of transactions (in the form of blocks) records to the public ledger of past transactions. The blockchain confirms transactions to the rest of the network as having actually taken place.

In order to add blocks to a chain, very complex cryptographic computations need to be computed. Upon the successful computation of each problem, the successful problem solver is rewarded with tokens of that blockchain (so in the case of bitcoin computations, the individual or group that solves the problem first is rewarded with bitcoins). These computations, which are basically math problems, become harder and harder and more and more complex with each subsequent block.

During the early periods of bitcoin development and mining, the cryptographic problems that needed to be solved in order to add a new block to the bitcoin blockchain were much easier than the problems of today. Mining could be done on a desktop computer. This meant that solving problems was easy, but the payoff was relatively small, because with each new block that was mined (more on mining below), the payoff of 50 or so bitcoins was probably worth just a few dollars.

As a result, and because the price of bitcoin was very low for so long, public adoption of bitcoin might have been easy, but there was no real commercial interest in it.

Miners from those times often look back now and wish that they had mined more, or kept the bitcoin they mined. The same is true for anyone who held any amount of bitcoin as recently as six or seven years ago, because if you bought $10 worth of bitcoin back in 2010 or 2011, those coins would be worth many hundred thousand dollars today!

Nodes

Because this is so important, we reiterate that the nodes of a blockchain are the computers on the network that contain the blockchain, which is the ledger of records of transactions. The miners are special nodes. Any changes happening in any one node are transmitted over the network. All changes are recorded in the blockchain. All nodes take part in verifying any transaction. The audit of a transaction conducted by one node is completely independent of any other node's audit. A vital feature of a blockchain is its regular and automatic updating, every few minutes. This updating process is not controlled by some centralized computer but is an inbuilt feature of the blockchain software.

A blockchain allows you to make secure online transactions. It does this by structuring digital records of transactions in database-form across many computers so that the record cannot be altered retroactively, without altering all subsequent blocks in the chain and having every node on the network agree to doing so. This structure allows all network and blockchain participants to verify and audit transactions safely, securely, and cheaply.

Decentralization is the process of redistributing or dispersing functions, powers, people or things away from a central location or authority and over all the nodes of the network that each have the blockchain.

Because transactions are only recorded permanently in the blockchain after they are authenticated by the nodes of the network, you end up with a robust workflow where you can confirm that a certain action has in fact taken place, and that it has taken place only once.

This is very important, as it helps to solve the problem of double-spending, where, for example, someone may promise to send funds to one person, and instead sends the same funds to multiple recipients before any single recipient can verify whether or not the funds have actually been sent or received.

Blockchain terms

The actual components of a blockchain consist of two kinds of records:

(i) Blocks and

(ii) transactions.

Blocks hold grouped batches of valid transactions, along with a pointer to the previous block in the blockchain, thereby linking the two inextricably. When you link blocks together, you form a chain (hence the name block *chain*). Repeating this process takes you all the way back to the first block, called the *genesis* block, and adding new blocks means your blockchain is growing in height.

*The **height** of a block on a blockchain is the number of blocks in the chain between the block in question and the genesis block (see below for the definition of the genesis block, which has a height of 0). Blockchain heights grow slowly over time, depending on the difficulty of the cryptographic computations required for the creation of additional blocks.*

*The **genesis block** of any blockchain is the first **block** in the chain. The genesis block is usually hardcoded into the software of the applications that utilize its **block**chain and the data contained therein is permanent and irreversible. All* *future transactions and data transfers are verifiably linked to the genesis block.*

Cryptography *is a scientific and mathematical process of preventing third parties or the public from reading private messages. It affects various things such as information security, data confidentiality, and data integrity, and can be used in digital communications, online commerce, and password securit*

Peer-to-peer *(P2P) computer networks are those in which various partitions of tasks or workloads are made between different users on the network. Each peer has the same privileges as everyone else on the network. Blockchain systems run on P2P networks.*

Peers make a portion of their resources, such as processing power, disk storage, or allowed bandwidth, available to other network participants, without having to resort to central coordination via server hosts. Collaborative P2P systems, such as blockchain, allow peers to do similar things, while sharing resources. They allow users to engage in more resource-intensive tasks, beyond those that can be completed by individual peers, yet are beneficial to all the peers.

*A **distributed ledger** (also called shared ledger) is a consensus of replicated, shared, and synchronized digital* *data geographically spread across multiple sites, countries, or institutions. There is no central administrator or centralized data storage.*

*A **hash pointer** is a cryptographic hash pointing to a data block. Hash pointers let you verify that the previous block of data has not been tampered with.*

Before finishing we mention that a hash is a mathematical function, which produces a strong of letters and numbers like *65ccae6c560387c3ae0b96df94c3e246bf1ef8971c5f67bbeacbe 66a25c6232c*

The mathematics and computing which produces this is not for the faint hearted!

Now that we know what blockchains are, how they are formed, why their specific properties are revolutionary, and the promise that this cutting-edge technology holds, let's now talk about actual benefits and implementations of blockchain technology to see just how its potential for transforming businesses and industries.

Chapter 4: Benefits of blockchain technology

The promise of blockchain sees all of the world's agreements and contracts digitized into code and stored in transparent, public databases, safe from being deleted, tampered with, or revised. In this scenario, every type of agreement, business process, online task, funds payment, and transactions of every type would have a single digital record that can be identified and validated. This would do away with middlemen such as lawyers, stock exchange brokers, and banks, saving billions, if not trillions, of dollars annually.

Blockchain is ideally suited to revolutionizing the way countless industries do business. Here is a brief list of some of the ways in which blockchain solutions will do this.

(i) *Doing away with third parties, and having exchanges that are not subject to trust* issues: Blockchain allows two or more parties to conduct an exchange of any sort they like, without having to resort to official oversight or intermediation in any way, shape, or form from an external party not directly involved in the exchange itself, which reduces or even eliminates counterparty risk.

Counterparty risk *is the risk to each party of a contract that the counterparty will not live up to its contractual* *obligations. Counterparty risk is a risk to both parties and should be considered when evaluating a contract. In most financial contracts, counterparty risk is also known as default risk.*

(ii) *Users are empowered and have control of their own data*: Have you ever thought about the fact that world's largest car services company (Uber) does not really own any of the cars that run its business, yet it rakes in billions via car rides logged by drivers using its app? Or how the world's largest home rental service (Airbnb) doesn't really own any of the properties it rents out, but it still collects commission for helping people locate places to stay? The same goes for Facebook (not creating any actual data but amassing data, marketing expenditure, and web visits from social shares by users), and other similar apps. With blockchain protocols in place, users own and are in control of all of their information and transactions themselves.

(iii) *Data quality and integrity*: With the blockchain, data is always complete (because the next block cannot be mined or created without being linked to a block that is verified as being complete in the chain), is consistent (all data necessarily has to conform to protocol standards, otherwise it would not be recorded in the chain), and is widely available (which is the main feature of decentralized systems such as blockchain).

(iv) *Durability and reliability:* Blockchain does not have any single point of failure and is able to withstand malicious exterior attacks more efficiently than closed systems with possible weaknesses and points of failure scattered throughout the system from within.

(v) *Integrity of data processing and transfers*: Because of the unchangeable nature of blocks in a blockchain, all users on the network can trust that all transactions that take place on the network are and always will be executed exactly, as the system is designed to do, removing the need for a third party to oversee transactions.

(vi) *Transparency and auditability*: All transactions to and on a blockchain are, by design, made on a public ledger that anyone can look at. There are various services, such as etherscan.io, that allow users to search for data, transactions, and to audit everything that is going on within and on a blockchain.

(vii) *Faster* transactions: Interbank transactions such as ACH (automated clearinghouse transactions) can take days to clear, especially for transactions made outside of working hours. Just think about sending a wire or making a purchase at the end of the business day on Friday, and being unable to see timely updates to the status of funds until as late as the following Tuesday or Wednesday. Blockchain transactions reduce transaction times to minutes and even seconds, and they are processed around the clock.

(viii) *Lower transaction costs*: Because there is no exterior party overlooking and supervising transactions, blockchains can potentially reduce transaction fees by a significant amount, leading to savings of billions of dollars annually.

Chapter 5: ICOs

Related to crowdfunding is the concept of initial coin offerings, or ICOs. ICOs are used by groups or companies that want to raise funds, and they use cryptocurrency to do so. Currently, ICOs are largely unregulated, and there is a lot of debate about whether or not the use of ICOs will stand the test of time, and whether or not using them is even legal.

In an ICO, investors fund a project by sending cryptocurrency to a designated project wallet. This makes ICOs different from initial public offerings, known as IPOs, because in an IPO, investors purchase shares in the company, but in an ICO crowdfund, investors buy coins of the company which act like stocks, and the value of the coins can appreciate in value if the project or business idea is successful.

The first ever token sale was held by a company known as Mastercoin, way back in July 2013. The Ethereum project raised money with a token sale in 2014.

ICOs have since become very popular. There were close to 20 coin offerings per month this year, with some ICOs generating tens of millions of dollars in funds in the space of a few minutes. There are also numerous websites that track ICOs, funds raised, and the value of coins, and this is information that investors find useful when deciding whether or not to invest in the next big cryptocurrency project.

One downside of ICOs is the frequency of hacks and thefts. There have been many costly phishing and Ponzi schemes this year, leading to the loss of millions of dollars for investors because of hacked wallets, and general scams that people unwittingly buy into, hoping for a big windfall. Regardless of the risk involved, there have been over 90 ICOs, so far in 2017, raising more than $1 billion overall.

When it comes to regulation, the U.S. Securities and Exchange Commission (SEC) said that not all blockchain ICOs would necessarily be classified as securities, but that such decisions would be made on a case-by-case basis. As of now, the SEC does not actively promote or endorse ICOs, a fact that has somewhat stymied the phenomenal growth of the cryptocurrency sector.

Currently, there are a lot of ICOs, and many of these can be seen on websites like *Coinschedule* or *ICOALERT*. If you are interested in them have a look at one of these sites.

Chapter 6: Existing industries being disrupted by blockchain technology

In the previous chapter, we revealed how ICOs are the method by which blockchain projects are being financed. Below are brief descriptions of a handful of successful and promising blockchain applications that have the potential to radically change various industries.

(i) *Smart contracts*: These are computer protocols that facilitate, verify, or enforce the negotiation or performance of a contract. They work by being automatically executed once certain conditions are met. Ethereum is a smart contract protocol that, like bitcoin, runs on blockchain, but in addition to containing transaction and timestamp data, ethereum contracts can also contain logic rules and conditions that can be executed by computer systems as soon as specific conditions are reached or met, meaning there is no backing out of such contracts, no cheating on them, and no unfair changes involved with them either. Ethereum has its own coin Ether (ETH), which is the cryptocurrency with the second highest market capitalization. In December 2017, this was more than $70 bn (US).

(ii)*Crowdfunding*: This is the practice of funding a project or venture by raising funds from a large number of people, and can be done by issuing contributors with digital assets for funding a certain initiative. In a way, it is like issuing stock to contributors, and the contributors then own a digital piece of the company or project that they funded and are entitled to profits from the initiative that come in the form of higher prices or higher demand for the digital token created by the project they funded.

(iii) *File storage*: Services such as **Storj** (pronounced 'storage') aim to provide cloud storage services that cannot be censored or monitored, and that have zero downtime. Storj is a platform, a cryptocurrency (meaning it is a digital asset created after a round of crowdfunding from the public), and a suite of decentralized apps (DAPPs) that allow users to store data on a public network of shared computer resources in a secure and decentralized manner. The blockchain features it uses include having a transaction ledger, public/private key encryption, and cryptographic hash functions (as described earlier) to ensure privacy and security. Further, it aims to be much, much cheaper (10 to 100 times so), faster, and more secure than, for example, AWS (Amazon Web Services) or other traditional cloud storage services. Storj is working diligently to solve data security issues with the help of its own web app called Storj Share, as well as Libstorj. Because it is a decentralized, end-to-end encrypted cloud storage that uses blockchain technology and cryptography to secure online files, it works without any need to trust a corporation, vulnerable servers, or hired employees with your files. Storj completely removes trust from the equation.

Similarly, **Sia** is a company that has issued the SiaCoin, and it leverages the capacity of blockchain technology to enable distributed networks to reach consensus in a secure and trustless way. Cryptographically secured smart contracts ensure that data encryption and transfer is conducted with no possibility for a third party to interfere in any way. Sia is a new approach to cloud storage platforms. Instead of all datacenters being owned and operated by a single company, Sia opens the floodgates and allows anyone to make money by renting out his or her hard drive. Data integrity is protected using redundancy and cryptography.

(iv) *Healthcare*: In the healthcare industry, we have **Patientory**. Patientory is a blockchain-based distributed electronic medical record storage computing platform. Healthcare entities can secure private health information, rent computing power, servers and data centers and make their unused resources available through a unique private infrastructure on the Ethereum blockchain. From the platform, smart contracts related to patient care can be executed.

Another healthcare blockchain service is **DentalFix**, which is a blockchain company for dental clinics and the supply chain related to dental work. The company was formed after merging two startups from the dental industry. They already provide professional software to more than 300 dental clinics worldwide.

Related to food quality and health we have **Ambrosus**. This project aims to combine high-tech sensors, blockchain technology, and smart contracts to build a publicly verifiable, community-driven ecosystem that assures the quality, safety, and eco-friendly origin of food and medicine products. Despite the fact that food and medicine are essential to everyday life, due to the inefficient and often dangerous way the world's global supply chain of input products is run, many people have no idea what they are consuming when they eat certain foods, or take certain pills or medications. The Ambrosus project aims to radically improve global supply chains. They plan to do this by creating a trusted ecosystem where users can reliably record entire product histories, and then execute private or commercial transactions based on that information. The hope is for this to lead to a more secure and autonomous supply chain, while bringing about improvements in distribution processes and allowing consumers to easily see where their products come from and what is really in them.

(v) *Energy*: In the field of energy, examples of the blockchain at work can be seen with **SunContract** and **TransActive Grid**. With SunContract, there is a platform that directly connects energy producers and consumers into an energy pool based on smart contracts. SunContract's vision is to support a global and self-sufficient energy community based on renewable energy by the digitization of electricity. With SunContract tokens called SNCs, you can buy electricity through the SunContract Energy Pool. SunContract's business model joins together the best features of blockchain technology (trust, transparency, traceability, time stamp, and transactions) and renewable energy (digitization, de-carbonization, deregulation, decentralization, and democratization) to create an entirely new service that is revolutionizing the existing energy market. Having decentralized energy markets on the blockchain is only the first step of transforming energy distribution grid services in the future and will be followed by grid-flow optimization services and demand -response services.

As for TransActive Grid, this service that is very similar to SunContract, in that it is a combination of software and hardware that enables members to buy and sell energy from each other securely and automatically, using smart contracts and the blockchain.

(vi) *The investment industry*: An example of a blockchain initiative in this field is **DCORP**. DCORP is an autonomous, decentralized, and democratic investment platform. It is an organization that exists on blockchain as a series of smart contracts. DCORP manages its own token (called DRP) and the Ether it holds. Anyone can join DCORP as shareholder or talented contributor anonymously through their Ethereum account. Shareholders are the collective owners of DCORP, and they collectively make decisions on business financials. The Board of Directors manages DCORP on a day-to-day basis, and they are all are elected and publicly known. All voting behavior is stored on the blockchain and thus made public.

Closely related to investments is stock trading. **Brickblock** is a project that aims to build a platform to seamlessly and transparently connect cryptocurrencies with real-world assets. Users are given the opportunity to invest out of cryptocurrencies into real-world assets such as stocks or real estate, and to receive regular dividend payouts as well. Additionally, this kind of crypto fund offers a great deal of diversification into many different cryptocurrencies with just one transaction.

Also in this field we have **Monaco**. This project recently released a Monaco VISA Card and touts itself as a must-have product for not only bitcoin and ether holders, but for anyone who ever has to spend money in foreign currency. One of the main features of Monaco's card is that it allows you to spend ether or bitcoin that you have in your possession with a physical Monaco VISA at all outlets and points of sale where VISA cards are accepted, both offline as well as online.

Only the exact amount that you spend with your card will be incrementally exchanged from between ether or bitcoin, in real-time, whenever you swipe your card, and the rest of your crypto assets are securely stored in your wallet - to which only you have access. You can also exchange money at exact interbank exchange rates using the Monaco app, which allows you to send money in 23 currencies to 120 countries worldwide, at no cost whatsoever. Whenever you use the Monaco app, the money sent and received is instantly deducted from you and available to the recipient on their Monaco VISA Card. If this is not a wild transformation of banking and currency exchange functions, then nothing else is!

(vii) *Research*: In the field of research, we have **Einsteinium**. The Einsteinium Foundation's mission is to raise funds for scientific research from a pool of funds that provide grants to deserving applicants. They recently integrated crowdfunding into the process to likely enable grant beneficiaries to receive more funds than could immediately be supplied. This enables the foundation to market projects, the Einsteinium coin, and to sponsor projects or ideas and to promote the benefits of cryptocurrency to a wider audience.

(viii) *Environmental conservation*: In the field of environmental conservation we have **EcoBit**, a company that is using blockchain technology to fund and fuel conservation efforts. A recent ICO held by EcoBit raised nearly $5 million, and that money was used to purchase pristine rainforest land in Malaysia. It was also used to create self-sustaining business ventures such as fish farming, coconut plantations, eco-tourism, and similar industries.

(ix) *Commodity trading*: Finally, an innovative example of a blockchain idea that is backed by an actual commodity is **ZrCoin**. This project leverages both cutting-edge financial and industrial technologies to manufacture and sell a highly in-demand product called synthetic zirconium dioxide (Synth. ZrO_2), which is traded on the global market. Owners of ZrCoins, ie. those who contributed to the ZrCoin crowdfund, are entitled to profits from the sale of the product, thereby connecting blockchain with an actual, in-use physical commodity.

These examples are by no means exhaustive. There are hundreds of different blockchain coins and tokens on the market, many of which are running successful products and companies, and many of which are being used to fund cutting-edge ideas.

Additional examples of blockchain projects beyond those described above include online prediction markets, insurance and reinsurance apps, decentralized online job marketplaces, cybersecurity tokens, blockchain-powered mobility apps, augmented reality combat games, indie TV series ideas, startup incubators, decentralized ad networks, e-sports that run on the blockchain, speech recognition platforms, safe and secure air ticketing projects, decentralized search, real-time strategy games, blockchain solutions for global freight, consumer microcredit services, identity verification on the blockchain, monetization of art on the blockchain, tokenized mobile data apps, blockchain-backed natural language processing for various types of biology projects, environmental conservation using funds collected via blockchain tech, decentralizing research and peer reviews, verifying publications, rewarding contributions to open-source projects (similar to Wikipedia, but rewarded in blockchain tokens), marketplaces for freelancers, cloud computing via blockchain, streamlining services of retailers and merchandizers on the blockchain, reducing company admin overheads by setting up and running smart contracts for everything from hiring and supply chain to closing sales and paying salaries (which is what **Aragon** is doing)...and the list is virtually endless.

Chapter 7: Further discussion about cryptocurrencies and tokens?

Is there a difference between cryptocurrencies and tokens?: There is not really any difference! As explained in chapter 5, tokens act as stocks or shares in projects funded by project contributors. These tokens are the coin that investors get in return for their investment. These coins are cryptocurrency and after the ICO will be treated as such on exchanges.

 Cryptocurrencies have dual functions: they can act as assets just like stocks, and they can also be used as a store for value, much like gold and silver. They can also be traded by users for ordinary goods and services. In fact, it was the possibility of having cryptocurrencies function as a medium of exchange that initially generated the most interest and investment to this new market.

However, it was also this feature that created obstacles to the cryptocurrency world. from world banks and governments, who did not want to see their stranglehold on world currencies and financial power reduced by decentralized and authority-free cryptocurrency solutions.

When talking about cryptocurrencies, the two heavyweights are bitcoin and ethereum. The difference between the two is that bitcoin is pretty much just a currency, and it acts as a store of value and can be traded for goods and services.

Ethereum, on the other hand, is an open-source, public, blockchain-based distributed computing platform, it features smart contract functionality, as explained earlier. It provides the Ethereum Virtual Machine (EVM), which can execute commands using a network of public nodes.

Ethereum has a cryptocurrency called *ether* which can be transferred between accounts and used to compensate participating nodes for computations that they perform. Ether is currently the second-most valuable cryptocurrency in terms of market cap, and it supports hundreds of projects that run on the ether blockchain. Many of these projects were described in the section above on disruptive blockchain projects reimagining countless industries today.

Another popular cryptocurrency is **litecoin**, which is a peer-to-peer cryptocurrency in which the creation and transfer of coins are based on an open-source cryptographic protocol and is not managed by any central authority, true to the central theme behind blockchain in general. While technically nearly identical to bitcoin, litecoin allows for more transactions to be processed by the network per unit time, reducing bottlenecks that are common with bitcoin. Litecoin also has almost zero payment cost and facilitates payments approximately four times faster than bitcoin.

There are many different examples of smaller currencies on the market. Bitcoin and litecoin are definitely the most well-known and popular ones, and with ethereum they carry the majority of the value of cryptocurrencies, but the many crypts described throughout this book all have distinct features and advantages, so they are each worth looking into individually.

One thing to know about cryptocurrencies is where they are stored, since there is no central authority that oversees the transfer, trade, exchange, or storage of cryptocurrencies. As such, investors who purchase coins in the market or invest in an ICO are expected to store their coins in an online or offline wallet. The next chapter deals with wallets.

Chapter 8: Wallets

*A **cryptocurrency wallet** is a secure digital wallet that is used to store, send, and receive digital currencies such as bitcoin or ether. Most run on an officially recommended wallet or a few compatible recommended third party wallets. Cryptocurrency wallets are needed to use cryptocurrencies, unless you only buy and sell on exchanges.*

Keep in mind, however, that your cryptocurrency is not actually stored in your wallet itself. Instead, a private key, which is a secure digital code that is known only to you and your wallet, is stored, and that indicates that you have ownership of a public key, which is a public digital code that is connected to a certain amount of currency. Because your wallet stores your private and public keys, it allows you to send and receive coins while retaining ownership throughout the trading process, and it also acts as a personal register of all transactions that you make.

Here is some information about wallets

A wallet for cryptocurrency is a secure digital creation that acts like a container for fiat money. What on Earth does this mean? **A wallet is actually a string of numbers and letters, such as 18c137626650e5550973303c500e136f22673b74.**The wallet is used for storing, sending, and depositing cryptocurrency. Some of the big cryptocurrency exchanges have wallets so that you can deposit the cryptocurrency you have bought through them, however, bear in mind that exchanges are often targets for hackers, so it is not generally recommended to keep your cryptocurrency there as there are some very clever hackers.

There are a minority of exchanges, Coinbase being one, that insure your coin at the exchange. However, it is best practice to store your money elsewhere using your own wallets.

Most cryptocurrencies have an official wallet. There are also some highly recommended wallets that are the products of third parties. No matter what your choice, it is essential that you have a wallet, if you wish to use cryptocurrency, most exchanges insist on this.

Wallets have two *keys*, a public and a private key. The public key is a string like 18c177926650e5550973303c300e136f22673b74. It is the address that those sending you funds use. The private key is also such a string, however, unlike the address you must never divulge it to anyone. You use the private key when you are sending funds.

Generally, it is recommended you use the official, or at least a wallet that has official blessing. Be careful as it has been known for 'wallets' to be malware. As an example, the GateHub wallet recently had to warn its clients about a fake Android app that was just a hack.

Treat wallets like email attachments and before you use a wallet be certain of its source. Wallets provide variable security. Some very good wallets use bio information, however, if you have never used this before it can be quite confusing. A very powerful security feature is multi-signature transactions. Other security features are being invented all the time and as you become experienced in cryptocurrency you will need to stay abreast of developments.

It is absolutely essential that wallets are backed up and a record of keys kept in a safe place. If you have the good fortune to have many coins then think about encrypting your keys.

I repeat, for proper security you need a minimum of one backup on an external hard drive of some sort, and it should not be connected to the Internet. As well as giving you the best defense from hackers it will be desperately needed if, by some mishap, the hard drive or your computer fails or is corrupted or erased. When you lose your wallet or keys, then you can farewell to the coin within! Don't put too much digital currency in any one electronic wallet. Have a number and don't put too much in any of them.

Here are some common wallets

(i) The desktop wallet: This is the most common wallet. Generally, it is an app that is connected to the coin's computer. A good example is the Jaxx wallet, which has Windows, Mac and Linux versions

(ii) Mobile wallets: These are similar to desktop wallets except that they run off a smart phone or tablet. There is nearly always an iOS version and an Android version.

(iii) Online wallets: With these, basically there is no software to be downloaded and installed because the wallet is in the cloud. Some online wallets make provision for the encryption of coin before entry in the wallet. As an example, the wallet *GateHub* is such a wallet.

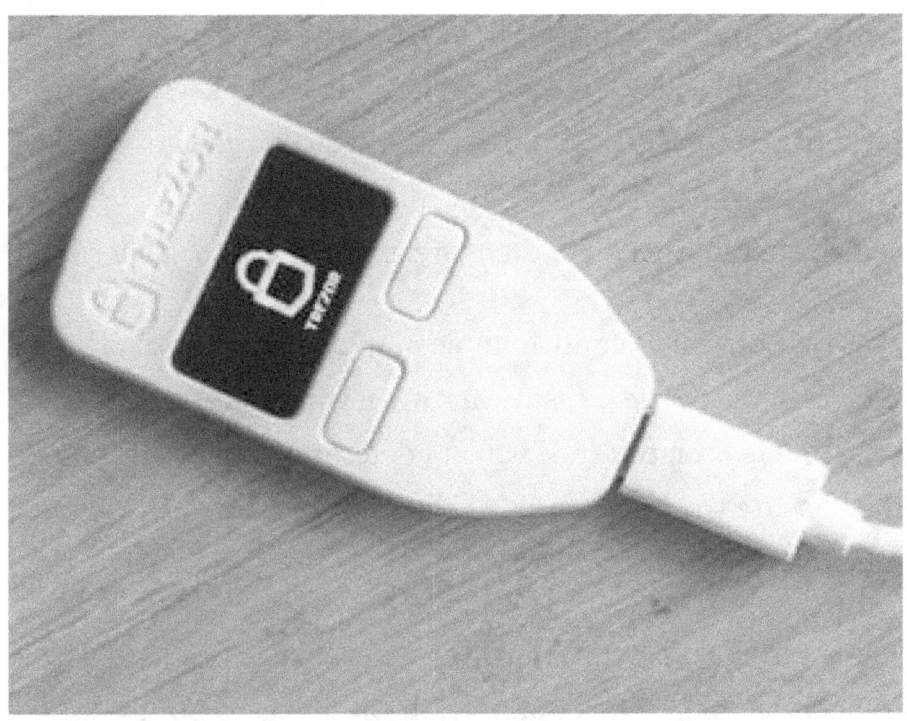

The safest wallets are hardware, they are not free but are the best for security when it comes to safe storage of cryptocurrency. Most hardware wallets are devices on a USB. See the diagram above of the well-regarded Trezor Wallet.

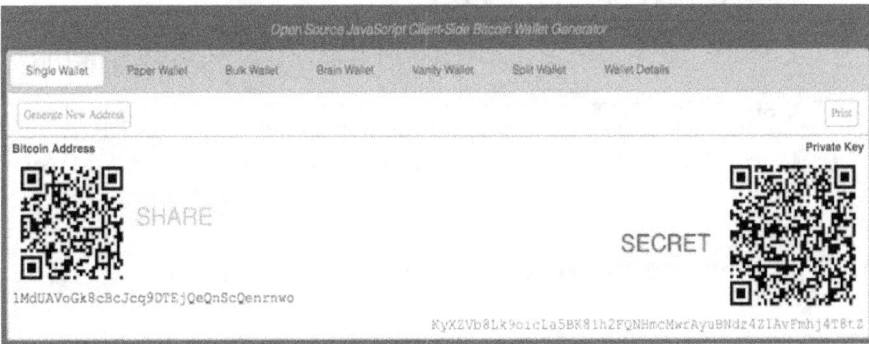

Lastly, Paper Wallets: These are incredibly simple and consist of QR codes, for both public and private keys, printed on paper. Have a look at the diagram. You can generate them yourself. A site that allows you to do this, is walletgenerator.net/ and there are a number of such sites.

This type of wallet, in my humble opinion, has all sorts of risks such as spilled coffee, frisky cats, open windows and general wear and tear on paper. If you are determined to use this type then ensure you have physically backed your keys up in some other way.

Transferring cryptocurrency from an exchange to a hardware wallet is simple. In this example, the exchange is Coinbase and the hardware wallet is KeepKey:

1. Plug in the KeepKey USB cable;
2. Open the KeepKey Client (It is under Apps, if you are using Google Chrome, however, could be somewhere else, with other browsers);
3. Locate the wallet's address on the the KeepKey Client's User Interface;
4. Using 'Send/Request' enter the wallet's address (public key).
5. Follow instructions before clicking 'Send Funds.'

It is always sensible to send a small amount first to ensure everything is working before sending a large sum.

Chapter 9: What are the risks and challenges of blockchain?

Currently, there is very little regulation with regards to what is and isn't allowed in the blockchain space. There have been numerous instances of hackers making off with millions of dollars of investor money because of loopholes in online blockchain systems. Despite the promise of security on the blockchain, there are teething problems which hackers are taking advantage of to the detriment of blockchain users.

For example, there was recently a case of Enigma, which is a decentralized platform that was preparing to raise money via an ICO. Enigma had its website and numerous social accounts hacked, and the attackers made off with almost half a million dollars, by sending out spam. The project was launched by a group of MIT grads, and what the attackers did was grab money from the Enigma community, people who joined the company's official mailing list or Slack group. All in all, they numbered over 9,000 users and participants.

The hacker posted messages on Slack, altered the official website, and spoofed emails to the community list to make it look like an official request for money. Money that was sent to the hacker's crypto wallet.

Similarly, but on a much grander scale, there was a huge $50 million hack last year when the Decentralized Autonomous Organization, or DAO, built on Ethereum, was hacked. The DAO was meant to be a decentralized investment fund in which decisions would not rest on a few partners, but instead, anyone who invested in the fund would have a vote in which companies or projects to invest in. The more you contributed, the more votes you had. And since the fund was built to be distributed, no one could take the money and run. However, due to human error and programming errors, hackers were able to exploit the system and make off with $50 million. This has not yet been recovered.

Here is another example: a company known as Gnosis recently sold $12.5 million worth of a token called GNO, in just over ten minutes. The sale, as is true for most ICOs, was intended to pay for the development of an advanced prediction market. The ICO received raving reviews across the global press.

On the same April day, over in Mumbai, India, a company called OneCoin was in the middle of a sales pitch for its own digital currency when their offices were suddenly raided by financial enforcement officers. Eighteen OneCoin reps were jailed, and over $2 million in investor funds were seized. Multiple authorities now described OneCoin, which touted itself as the next bitcoin, as a Ponzi scheme, and by the time those Mumbai offices were raided, the company had already moved at least $350 million in scammed funds.

Because there are no checks and balances governing the execution of ICOs, if you are going to invest in a coin, you need to make sure it's not just any random idea that could just be a scam.

There are major hurdles in the way of formally legalizing and regulating crypto trades. With market growth and adoption, similar challenges exist. What kinds of tax structures are right for blockchain markets? How can funds be traced and aggregated? Where and how will spending and income information come from? As long as these issues remain question marks on the policy boards of decision-makers, widespread adoption of blockchain will be difficult.

However, there is some promise: Japan and South Korea have recently made major advances in allowing for legal bitcoin transactions, and various applications have opened investment channels in the blockchain space to traditional investors, which has led to an influx of funds to different blockchain companies, which have in turn been able to invest in growth, research, and promotion of their blockchain services.

To summarize, these are the risks of blockchain technology.

- It is a new technology, so resolving challenges such as transaction speed, the verification process, and data limits is a major challenge standing in the way of making blockchain widely adopted.
- The regulatory status of blockchain projects is uncertain, and cryptocurrencies are a totally different ballgame from modern currencies that have always been created and regulated by national governments. Blockchain faces a major hurdle in widespread adoption if financial institutions and governments don't buy into the idea, or if they are pushed away by a lack of clear guidelines on how the industry should be regulated.
- Mining is highly energy intensive, and if we look at bitcoin, it is becoming even more expensive with each new block on the blockchain. There may be a limit to how much miners are willing to spend on solving mathematical puzzles to earn a few bitcoins as a reward for mining the next block.
- There are also cybersecurity and integration concerns that need to be addressed before the general public will willing entrust their personal data to a blockchain solution. The same goes for getting the green light from any body of users or a Board of Directors to make significant changes to, or even completely replace, any existing system.

- Finally, there is the issue of social and cultural adoption. Blockchain represents a complete shift to a decentralized network which requires major buy-in of all users and operators on the network, and it is such a major development that is not really understood very well by a lot of people, so it will take some time, perhaps years, before we see widespread adoption of blockchain solutions across the board.

Chapter 10: Are cryptocurrencies a good investment?

Some people compare the crypto market with winning the lottery. Although there are often major swings in the cryptocurrency world, swings that make millionaires overnight, the comparison is not entirely accurate, because long-term investing in numerous areas, projects, companies, or coins, is what will make money for you over the long run. This is very different from speculative day-trading, which is somewhat similar to gambling.

What day-traders do is make educated guesses at how a specific investment or group of investments will perform on a short-term basis. 'Short-term' may be a few days, or even a few minutes. The goal is not to simply keep up with the performance of the market or economy as a whole; rather, the goal is to make a lot of money and get rich quickly. The fact remains, though, that even though there are numerous bitcoin and ehtereum millionaires, the prices of cryptocurrencies regularly often swing from one extreme to another. For example, a recent crash on a particular exchange saw the price of ether drop from over $300 to just 10 cents in one day!

Notwithstanding the capricious nature of the crypto market, many things still hold true for it. You can invest wisely in it by buying low and selling high; there are numerous options from which to choose, backed by real projects with measurable deliverables and bottom lines; there may be limited safety protocols and risks of hacks, but you can still operate safely if you keep up to date with market developments and are smart about storing, transferring, and exchanging your tokens.

As far as investment advice is concerned, the bottom line is this: there are plenty of get rich quick schemes, but they rarely work out well. Don't invest anything you cannot afford to lose, read and learn however much you can, invest wisely, and experiment until you know what you are doing. Slow and steady wins the race.

Conclusion

As stated in the introduction, there have been few inventions over the course of history that have really made long-lasting and dramatic impacts on the direction and pace of human progress.

Blockchain promises to be one such invention. The promise it holds for transforming healthcare by providing safe and secure medical records, the possibility of redefining air travel, ocean freight, and global logistics using blockchain-backed solutions, the opportunities in the fields of finance, microfinance, credit, investments, and prediction markets that use decentralized protocols, and the proven capability of having cryptocurrencies that run on blockchain tech act as stores of value and media of exchange, all suggest that the world is slowly waking up to what blockchain to do.

However, there is still a lot of work that needs to be done. Millions of dollars of investment are being poured into this area of research and development, and every day there are new blockchain-based ideas, startups, and initiatives being launched, each one hoping to be the one that will catch fire and transform the way things are done. The time for change is now, and blockchain is powering the drive to change, but we should take cautious steps while moving forward to ensure we use the technology in the right way and deliver as much benefit to as many people it as possible through it.

DEAR READER,
THANK YOU FOR BUYING AND READING MY BOOK!
IF YOU LIKE IT, PLEASE, LEAVE A REVIEW. IT IS
IMPORTANT FOR ME AND MY FUTURE BOOKS.
JUST SCAN THIS QR CODE AND YOU CAN LEAVE A
REVIEW

OR JUST TYPE THIS LINK –
HTTPS://WWW.AMAZON.COM/REVIEW/CREATE-
REVIEW?IE=UTF8&ASIN=B078GWQ5G5#